Dunes

musings from 40 days in our desert

Dunes

musings from 40 days in our desert

anjali sebastian

WINCO
BOOKS

First Published by Winco Books
(An Imprint of Winco Publishers)
Kottayam 686575, Kerala, India
wincobooks@gmail.com
wincobooks.com

First Edition 2020

DUNES
Musings from 40 Days in Our Desert
By Anjali Sebastian

2191431520066

Cover design and layout by Winco Publishing Services

Printed and bound in India

USA – US $10 | India – ₹200

For my steady rays of sun and gusts of wind,
who help me
see clearer,
move lighter,
and be better:
P, L, and J-TSK

We don't have to do it all alone.
We were never meant to.
— **BRENÉ BROWN**

Although we've come
to the end of the road
still I can't let go
it's unnatural
you belong to me
I belong to you.
— **BOYZ II MEN**

And you?
When will you begin that long journey into yourself?

…The wound is the place where the light enters you.
— **RUMI**

Contents

III. Intermission

IV. Hip-Hop Hope: Digesting the Globe

V. Temp Swan Song: Shaker of the Globe

Foreword

Walking through the pathway to Life in the Spirit in the company of someone two generations younger than me is a unique experience. Challenges arise. Differences in perspectives can distort perception. But when each party genuinely seeks understanding, and if each one is willing to let unnecessary barriers fall, a new perspective can emerge.

Anjali Sebastian titled her book of poetry *Dunes*. I find that appropriate. Sand dunes are both beautiful and potentially dangerous. There's more to them than meets the eye. The visual beauty is obvious, but quasi-sink holes sometimes occur when you least expect it. In forming new relationships, there is always a temptation to reduce people to what we know about them.

Of course, according to the late psychiatrist Rudolph Allers, a student of Jung, "A man is what a man does." But everything he does is based on his thoughts, his dreams, his fears, his memories, the bad things and the good things he has done, his successes and failures, his frustrations, his prayers, his loves, his choices. How little we really know about each other!

My mother used to say, "It takes all kinds of people to make a world." Diversity should be celebrated like so many facets of a crown jewel. In the wake of 88 years of life, I would add that it takes the best part of a lifetime to really know anyone, especially ourselves.

Love commands intuition and enables the lover to reach the less obvious identity strata within the beloved. This treasure could be in the form of potential talent or primal goodness. Intuition is a gift not given equally to everyone. How often have we heard or thought, "What does she see in that guy?"

Such a discovery can be a source of significant joy and elation. While reading *Dunes,* I felt the poet's openness to wonder and delight in all the people and events of life. Is this the prerogative of youth alone? I think not. I hope not.

Even as Anjali witnesses to her being "moved" by our exchanges, so am I when I take the time to tone down the audio of creaking joints and lay aside the stack of obituaries to once again relish in the exuberance of life.

Dunes is delightful: life seen through the prism of youthful innocence, a sensitive interplay of a keen intellect, amazing intuition controlled by rhythmic patterns. Perhaps, some of this talent can be explained by the early influence of her Eastern cultural heritage. Somehow, Anjali learned how to listen to her spirit and to the music of the Cosmos.

Keep an eye on this young poet/songwriter. If she can produce work of this quality as a teenager, what might we expect when she is in full bloom?

I hope reading this little volume will reawaken the time when you, too, dear reader, were eighteen, or simply youthful and hopeful.

Janet A. Gelineau Keating, M.A.

Preface

As you breathe in this oxygen,
my hope is that you experience your life anew.

For my greatest hope is that you'll come to better know
your loved ones, the ones around you, and most
importantly,
                                yourself.

                        We can catch more flies with honey
                                than a SWAT team.

Read this as poetry,
build on these lyrics,
feel these musings,
and/or hear this music.

However you choose to intake,
share your outtakes, and
partake in real conversations.

All I ask is that you take this off the pages
and live fresh with it.

I

Journey Journals: Trapped in a Snow Globe

To be alone with one's thoughts is to be surrounded.
To be locked in one's imagination is to be liberated.
To be astray is the opportunity to be discovered.

Day 1

the call

I am alone
and I am crowded.

I am lost
and I am immersed.

I am concentrate
and I am dispersed.

I am last
and I am first.

It took me eighteen years to realize
that I have untapped
impact.

Who am I?

God lent me, no self-interest,
40 days to find out just that.

But more so,
to act.

Day 2

inquiry

Fell asleep on my bed,
now I awake in my head.

Where am I?

Wisps of saffron line my eyes,
lyrics of hair graze my jaw,
back flat on the earth,
sand dances on my skin.

Buried alive? Or barely alive?

Blink only to find
the fireball in the sky answer: home.
Swelling heat urges me to stand.
Cacti pierce my temples.
Parched—from lips to hands.
Who knew consciousness was fickle?

Can it be too loud if there are no sounds at all?

Home used to never be this painful.
Home was never this lonely.
Is this home?

I don't know.

Day 3

baby steps

Today, I take my first step.

Timid at first.
        light dip. okay.

Overconfident the second.
        deep dip. oof.

I settle for trepidation for the third try
onwards.

What??
As long as I'm moving forward!

I couldn't stay back there.

Day 4

feeling it

I walk in a perpetual forward lean
as if a reflection pool is about to appear
and quench my desire to know who I am.

I drag the balls of my feet.
And for the first time in a while,
I gaze down at my hands.

The poor, cracking things.
They're not used to being unused—
after years of playing the keys and
yoga practice and praying for my path
to be made clear to me,
this drab swinging has them confused.

Emerald rivers of veins coast down them
from wrist to knuckles.
Sand particles catch my eyes—the suckers.

Everything in sight is nothing at all,
but it's something I must surmount.

I still move with trepidation.

At least I can think that out loud—
mouth too dry to speak, to even make a sound.

Day 5

coulda, shoulda, woulda

Listen.

　　　　　Listen to understand.

I hear my Ma's voice saying this, like she has
so many a time before.

Right now, I think of my mother—miles away from me.
She always says enjoy the journey—
though I don't think she digests her own advice ever.

But that does not mean she is not right.
She most always is.

Though maybe I don't take that advice to heart either
because I've heaved and broken my back
every
day
of my existence.

And ever since I woke up in this desolate isolation,
my mind has run rampant,
and I am not present.

I'm not being as present as I could be.

> "Coulda,
> Shoulda,
> Woulda."

Another one of my darling mother's mantras.

Day 6

the gift of now

In an effort to relish in the gift of now,
I smile at the tan horizon.

The dips and rises of the fireball
and the grains of sand

      cascade

           across the space

like a masterful work of art.

Like street dance, like ballet,
like a song written, like gallery displays.

I couldn't have imagined it as I am.

As I move,
I'm operating at eye-level.

Am I missing scenes of the greater picture?

Day 7

the snow

God has a fair share of trinkets.

Surprises?

Jokes?

Whatever it is,
it is always sensational.

Enter: powdered sugar from the dome sky.
My Manna from Heaven.

Did you know it can SNOW in the desert?
In this globe?

The flakes take me to easy times.

And that's the immune boost I need to go further.

To dig deeper.
To own up.

God knows.

Day 8

the eye, the gem

Easing into this journey means
absorbing what is and isn't there.

I stop in what seems like
the middle of this desert—
the pitcher's mound, the eye of the hurricane.

Where everybody and nobody
has to and cannot wait for my next move.
Whew! What a view, and what not a view.

This world is a lot
BIGGER
less reachable,
and *less meaningful*
when I'm the only one in it.

As I see and hear more,
I realize that everywhere
has the elements of a wasteland—
no matter how beautiful.

Until,
one gem radiates
one gem steps up
one gem reflects
and, all in due time,
life, purpose, is restored
and we feel the effects.

Day 9

bound by time

Shins splinting.
Eyes glinting with
tears of sweat.

Body missing
the spirit of
a tangible home.

Is it right to be this alone?
For this long?
How long has it been—
out here?
How long has it been since:
I knew another's touch?
I knew the taste of food?
I took a sip of water?

Time,
what a wild bound.

Free, but not unlimited.
Fleeting, but not inhibited.

Sands of time,
take me to where and who I seek.

Day 10

the root and the soil

As I open my door
to some songs of humanity,

I dream of
Love.

The root of all goodness.

The soil of our deeds,
intentions,
words,
and nonverbal,
and active expressions.

To know love
is one thing.

To be love
is another.

It's easier
to respect the ones
with whom
we could share
potential love.

It is easier to love the ones who love us back.

It is trying, however,
and, most days, seems nature-defying,
to love absolutely everyone.

How and where to begin…

II

Folk Song: Folks' Stories: Exploring the Globe

intro

Folks' stories flock my mind sporadically,
unchronologically,
on this humdrum walk.
For at the end of the day,
my muses fuse together
and all I see is me and all I see is you.
And even then, the line that separates us
is low visibility, foggy, hazy.
Is this a mirror?
For I see my brothers, my lovers, my sisters,
all in you.
How are we even different?
My muses fuse together.

How many dreams have we hit snooze.

What booze do we drown in
when we don't choose the right river.

It's old news that we can elevate
through the experiences of others.
As long as we let in and
then allow these stories to fester,
and attest to

the strength and weakness
we don't know we have within.

As the sun rises, still,
my muses fuse together and all I know is me
and **all I care to know**
is you.

Day 11

super children

She's a wonder,
a wandering, meandering star.

At seven years old,
she's the essence of youth.
And I know she'll still be
when she has the time to read this.

She's the kind of person who notices
everything before you ever will.
She runs barefoot and cannot stay still.
Her favorite question is "why?"
and no answer will suffice
for the mind of the most
imaginative child I know.
She struts down the street
with the most inspired hairdos,
dresses, and makeup.

Then, she breathes that life into the
inanimate—leaves, acorns, rocks, chalk,
and dust.

And then she joins me,
her walking buddy,
her talking buddy—
we're sisters, we pretend for real.

She's curious, a mindful handful.
She's a neighbor, an up-close entertainer.

I want to be like Olivia when I grow up.

* * *

This is for a Baby grand,
a three-year-old hero.

Stronger than cancer,
stronger than chemo.

Though your hammers are
unjustly tampered with,
the way you play
lights up a room—

you are the best song.

Maker of
the flyest sample beats.
Wired for dancing—
you cute!

Bossy baby,
baby Boss—
child of
the most
elite caliber,
and character—

the most precious cargo.

Day 12

a guru

Back home
in the suburbs
of northern Texas,

Janet, 88, February, blue eyes, writes about her life.
As a nun,
turned wife,
then mother,
all for her grandchildren.

The simplicity
and the clarity with which she lives
moves me.

Changing vocations
and living the Truth,
a Liberal Catholic,
she guides my youth.

The simplicity
and the clarity with which she speaks
moves me.

The daughter of a French-Canadian Borden's truck driver
and nurse, born up in Michigan.
Rose as a teacher, a contemplative, a seer, a fighter.

The love
and the faith with which she moves
moves me.

Day 13

the agent of change

My mind leaps
to the grass-hooper,
the changer of my life,
the refiner of my menu.

This is for the one who
puffs out his chest
and gave his best to
a nine-year-old dreamer.

For I saw the world in a year and a half
and only understood the gift later
(as I write this).

Whether it be hammering away
on the silky black keys,
bouncing the ball for hours
in the playroom,

truly helping me like no man had before,
or giving me a heaven to bloom,

you were the white horse that resurrected this child.

Strawberries, bunnies, cockroaches, sundials.

There isn't a word I could say or write to sum you up,
but I was blessed to feel the way you love.

Day 14

the faithful

"For the sake of
His Sorrowful Passion,"

she prays in her glorious, delicate voice
from the front pew of the chapel.

Shawl on her neck,
beads in the crook of her hand.

She leads the rosary
totally
in reverence
of the above dimension.

> Imagine if all creation were like her.
> And maybe we are.

Final bead 50,
she sings: "For the sake of His Sorrowful Passion."

And, ohh, the way her voice cracks
has me weak in the knees.

> I would fall on my knees,
>   if I weren't already kneeling.

Oh, how I admire this sweet, elderly lady
all the way from pew 3.
I don't know her name,
but, for Christ's sake,
she gets me.

Thank you, Jesus,
for this glimpse of Divine Mercy.

Day 15

brother

Brother,
no one else could get away
with being a once-a-month
Popeye's treat.

                    Only you.

January 1997. April 1999. August 2001.
I don't know if I could have planned it better.

             I always wanted a big brother.

Even though you wore your watch
too high for my taste,
and pulled your socks up
too high for your age,
and left me in a field to face
what I could not know,

we bonded over Star Wars II:
you watched it three times in one day that one time
for me.

We snacked on cheese puffs, the white cheddar kind.

It was sublime.
I had a fine time hanging out with you.

We had a 180 after 360,
and I think we came to an understanding.

                              I don't know if you miss me,
                                     but I miss you.

Day 16

bubba

Friday Market, to the desert, to Frankfurt, to Texas.
My traveled, cultured boy.

You are every great thing.

Anyone who has been blessed
by your kisses knows that you have
magic within.

You howl the best harmonies—
you crooner you.
Harmonizer to the synthesizers: colonizer of my heart.

Swede, sweet and savory
coconut cream with streaks of Kashmir snow,
corduroy Theodore, as I hug you, you let out your
signature grumble snore.

Oh! And you got eyeliner eyes without even trying.

Valentine, Pal-entine
    Baby Mine
        My nimble Boo
            Scorpio King
                Bubba Ghanoush.

I don't know personal space when it comes to you.
I don't and won't ever know someone like you.

We've been through everything together;
I'm filled to the brim.

And maybe you can't read this, but,
I love you intensely and infinitesimally.

Only a *few* days separate us now.

Day 17

the maestro

In person or via Skype,
despite distance, despite time,
you really supported the music in me.

When you used to play your own classical compositions,
or teach me Khachaturian,
or arrange Sare Jahan Se Accha for me even though you're
Armenian and I'm Indian
(music knows no borders),
or vibe with "DJ Got Us Falling in Love Again" by Usher,
I realized how rare a teacher you are.

I still remember the lesson
when you told me that rap
stands for rhythm and poetry—
and that's all I've lived by since then.

The picture frozen in my memory
is you at the keys,
fingers and wrists as strong as the shapes of 1 & 7,
the piano embracing you.

You're playing your "Seeds of Pomegranate,"

and a miracle *snow* dances all around.

Day 18

mama

18 years ago, you gave birth to me.

I could try to write your story in a
one-page poem,
but we both know you've had too many struggles
for one woman to endure.

Plus, there have been so many metaphors
and déjà vu and coincidences.

Ma, isn't it funny how the smallest things
trigger the next, or correlate
to a much greater event?
And I know you would say: "what's *funny* about it?"

Thus, I would simply go on
for much too long
because your story is never-ending—
you will live on through me and sis.

And I may have children just so
you can live on through them.

Simply put,

                love is my mother.

See, she knows what we need even before we all think it.
She, she is my hero.
Please, never judge her. Or anyone, for that matter.

Love is my mother
and compassion is her story.

Day 19

the bud

Friendship is like the
person you see in the mirror every morning—
it looks different by day,
it evolves through years.

Sometimes it's good food that links two people.
Ours were snacks n' sushi.
Sometimes it's movies,
and rolling on the floor laughing.

We would play and pause movies
just to replay scenes and repeat laughs
and imitate impressions. We thought
we were impressive.

You had a lasting impression on me.

When biking was our main mode of transport,
before we learned to drive,

we dreamed of flying: you like in Marvel,
me to California, us to Monte Carlo.

Some connections are as easy as the wind,
and steady as warmth on a sunny day.

Some connections are special
and especially smooth—

   don't let them slip away.

Day 20

sis

I think of you, my darling sister.
The story of a simple folk I know complexly well.

I think you know the most of my quirks.
I'm coming to you "live" to let you know:
likewise.

You a G.O.A.T, sis,
with your oat milk froth
and all the groceries you've bought
for me, the one who can't handle stores.

Your house slippers and
chocolate cake cravings,
and how you never actually hear what I'm saying,
but still manage to know most Bollywood lyrics—
roll my eyes, God forgive me.

You've pulled my leg since my beginning
and we'll have jokes until the end.

You have many intolerances, but
you haven't been too intolerant of me.

I spot a Manitou incline ahead,
like the steep climb of our old relationship
until we accepted our differences.

Here in this desert, I don't got energy for this.
There's no one around to share these concerns with,
except the Lily I speak to in spirit.

I imagine you sigh:

"Godspeed, my friend."

III

Intermission

—A pause in the music, a break in the shuffle—

(Inspired by Dharma Productions)

IV

Hip-Hop Hope:
Digesting the Globe

intro

Here comes the **beat drop**.
The climactic escape from the sphere comes from
the gained perspective of understanding.

Picture a world where we understand
the *gravity* of each moment *as it is happening,*

a world where we *really* walk with each other
for this journey belongs to all of us,

a world where we wish only greatness
upon others and we *actually intend* for
that greatness to blossom—

this all *could* be the world in which we live.

For now, this climax is not an action sequence.
I'm at a standstill, on the tallest dune yet:
reflecting rays and digesting.

Day 21

just be

If I am the reason you wake up today,
start un-training yourself
because I won't be here forever.

It's easier to adjust the lever
of your mind now than to
pull the weight of regret later.

I love you, I do.
And I don't naturally
think like this, I don't.

But this axis of time we're all
balancing on unveils my gravest fear:
losing you.

So, do me a favor:
love me deeply right now.

And I'll feel the ripples of our unconditionality
on every occasion.

Wake up in faith.
Live on your terms.
And love me as well as you can.

No fear.

Wake up in faith.
      Live on your terms.
            And love me as well as you can.

Day 22

too short, too long

Though this time we have
runs out at no one's pace,
I won't write my minutes off.

I will dwell in the story endowed on me:
from the footnotes to the dog-eared pages.
I will own my tale.

You and you and you—you must own yours,
or at least pick up where you left off.

Every morning,
        we go to school,
                we go to work.

And often
we are more busy than productive,
more "getting through it" than "going for it,"

more waiting for better, instead of making better now,
more drained than fulfilled.

Let's rewire this cycle,
we can go for the gold—
Tour de France style.

> *Existence is too short*
> *once you find what you're living for*
>
> *and too long*
> *without a purpose.*

So, shall we believe in us
and then believe in something
greater than ourselves?

> *Existence is far too short*
> *once you find what you're living for*
>
> *and far too long*
> *without a purpose.*

Day 23

lift off

These are the hands of
a working woman,
a striving woman.
You can feel my calluses,
but not the deep ones.

My deep ones come from
knowing that however I struggle,
my mother handled more—
my trials pale in relation.

I was bred on Ship 23,
on the launch pad, because of the
working hands of the
women before me.

They said,
"now, we've brought you here,
so that…"

Then, my foremothers gave me
a telescope and said,
"…look, you can transcend this sphere."

Enveloped in duvets of color,
I can and I will.

Wrapped in wings,
we can and we will
                              lift off.

Day 24

art is

When you move from
dune to dune
mindlessly,
it's easy to miss the in-between.

But art is in the in-between.

Art is in the sinking—

in the

humbling
        valleys.

Day 25

flow

It is true!
We have one mouth,
and two ears, so yes!
Listen more than you speak.

Alas,
do not forget the channels
between:

your ears and your mouth
your ears and your heart
your ears and your mind

your heart and your mouth
your mind and your mouth

and maybe most importantly,
your heart and your mind.

Hear! Hear! Aye! Aye!

Day 26

not knowing

Things are easy to know
and simple to practice.

Simple is not easy.

Life is only
rife with challenges
when we do not know
what we do not know.

This kind of not knowing
is the most complicated of all.

Day 27

excellence

I was treated differently
than the person next to me
most of my life—
from the once-over looks,
to the disinterested body language,
to my words that they cut short,
my accomplishments dismissed,
and the opportunities not extended.

I am a woman, divinely colored brown.
And yet, the majority of minorities
knows how this goes.
So, I extend my arms to you,
bearer of unequal burden.

I've learned that undeniable excellence supersedes
limits and labels imposed on us.
It should not have to be this way.
It is not fair that we've had to feel this way.

But I want you to know
that you are excellent.

And you have the capacity to prove it.

Dear anyone who has not experienced discrimination,
please be the light, even if you were raised in darkness.
Let at least one person know each day
that they are not lesser than.

Share unprecedented love
with everyone breathing—

                                 we breathe the same air.

Day 28

next steps

Consider

that the single balloon in the sky
is the new message in a bottle—
the signal that the lone wolf
next door

just needs a call.

Ring the doorbell,
ring their cell.

If they don't answer,
it does not mean they do not
still need your help.

Take the next step.
Bring together a pack,
confide in your tribe.

Go to the forest, ·
and listen for the howl.

The moon will light the way:
do not be afraid
to go the distance.

Day 29

solutions

There are people, just like you and me,
who go without water right now,
who do not even get to decide
between dine-in or take-out,
who go to bed
without a roof over their dreams,
who wake up
on concrete streets
without blankets, on sheets of ice.

Children who have never had any
sort of education,
and don't have anyone
who cares enough to wonder
how they are.

Sometimes these souls are as close as
one block away from us.

Why do we insist on discussing the pointless?
When this is the point: we are in a global crisis.

When we haven't had anything
meaningful to miss,
we settle for the petty things.

Think, instead of doing X, I will:
reach out and
how to be a part of the solution
will be made known to me.

Day 30

invest

Stock market plunging
and yet we're still floating
and there is still poverty.

If we are trillions in deficit
and we still have all we need,
why didn't we put this money
in a global fund that would
uproot every country
out of poverty?

Chump change,
for the suits with big pockets,
for real change.
Imagine it—"big names for big change."

Personal wealth is transient.
And at the end of the day,
monetary value is arbitrary.

There has got to be a reason why
we are all here at the same time.

Invest in the globe's wellbeing.

Day 31

your people

I remember where
I was standing when
you walked
away

and did not look back.

I looked down
at my feet
and thought
what's so wrong with me
that these feet could never
walk away from
someone who needed me.

Never trick yourself
into thinking that you are the problem,
when deep down you know
someone else fell short.

You're more tenacious than you know.

Trust your gut and
live in love
with the wisdom that
the people who adore you to your core
and deserve your energy
will strengthen you
by standing by you and

will not walk away.

Day 32

the trenches

You've been stuck
on substances,
and locked in your head.

I could advise you with the substance
in the words of Alicia Keys
or Oprah or Gandhi or Shakespeare,
and yet those are the doses you just don't take to.

But making you get it
is not my job.
I've tried.
You lied when you said you
care about me and my time.

Being in your alley's like
here's my pocket, you can pick it.
here's my heart, yuh, you can rip it.

I'm mugged in a way,
here I am unplugged all the way.
Hand you the aux cord
you say nahh, I got Bluetooth.
Yeah? Well, I got white teeth,
watch me bare them now,
because I can't stay silent any longer.
I will not be walked all over any longer.

I'm not blaming or attacking you.
I've just gleaned that I'm not going to
start a battle with you in the trenches—

I have work to do
and a war of love
to inflict
out there.

Day 33

crosses

I choose to not be bogged down
by what I
cannot control.

Sandstorms have roared
in this desert of ours.
They've shaken me,
but why should I
fear, or get hung up?

Winds gust at their own tempo,
and so, I must.

There will be
nonstop arguments
and unknowns.

So, I'll bear my crosses,
but no, I won't be cross with you.

I must conserve my energy for
the real fight—
however it manifests.

So, until then, I will bear my crosses,
but no, I will not be cross with you.

Day 34

care

Nurture
the one
inside

so that you can notice
the one
beside you.

To all the diligent
caretakers
everywhere,
who give every part of themselves
to everyone who does and does not ask,
you are veterans of living tender and
we don't ever wanna hurt you,
and we don't ever wanna change you.

Caregivers,
tend to yourselves—

ask someone else to massage your feet

because they likely won't notice,
like you would,

that you need it
like you do.

Day 35

real hope

I won't presume
to know what you
have been through.

All I can tell you
is what I understand now,
atop this dune.

Forgive me,
if I have not yet encountered your
struggle—

I know there is *much more* to come,
beyond the scope of my musings.

Enlighten me,
please.
Join me,
for some tea.

We'll set up a tent on this
very vantage point,
with what materials I do not know,
but I do need to know your story.

The human condition is *ups and downs*.
Ergo, your *constant* courage
through your *authentic* experiences
will give me **real hope**.

V

Temp Swan Song: Shaker of the Globe

intro

For now, I leave you with some
lullaby musings as I make my way toward the
desert night's horizon.

You are *the wielder of the key,*
the portal to the future.
You are *the shaker* of the snow globe,
and of the globe indeed.

Watch the magic dance,
and let the music play.

You have infinite power for good within you:
tap into it.

My hope is that these gentle assurances
and reassurances will lift your spirits.

Keep on journeying:
meditate,
restore, repose.
Though the heart breaks one too many times,
the *soul* will *not* crumble for
healing transpires all along the way.

I love you, love.

Day 36

grape juice

Say, you drinkin' grape juice
in a wine glass.
Hiding what's inside,
you won't last
out there,
in here,
I promise you that

I'll love you
once you love you.

Be willing to
love yourself
and the journey will follow.

I'll love you
once you love you.

Oh, how you may have no idea that
the one with the real power
is you.

Day 37

heart

Lub dub, lub dub.
The drum in your chest
is your compass.

And though it is often
torn between *at least* two directions,
it is not pointless.

Surely, it is leading you
where no one and nothing else can
fathom you can go—

out of the cage and off the beaten road.

Day 38

audacity

By default,
higher risk
allows for the chance
of higher return.

Thus, I shouldn't worry
when I take a chance,
risk it all for you,
and you can't return my love.

For then I'll know that my bravery
is independent of you.

Day 39

intertwine

How blessed are we
that sometimes,
at the right moment,
we say exactly what
someone needs to hear,
right then and there.

How blessed we are
that we can motivate
someone to go the distance,
before we are even
particularly close with that someone.

The nature of our connection
is wildly intertwined:
you and I,
we have most feelings in common,
though we experience them
separate.

Envision it—
all the babies we will raise,
all the humans we can mentor.
How will we teach them
to see the sun
despite the dips, throughout the peaks?

Oh, all the women, men, and beings you'll grow.
Bask in the light they shed.

I salute you,
with rays of praise,
for the time and energy you put in for our tomorrows.

Day 40

desert the notion

As the night falls
and stars engrave themselves
in the midnight-blue sky,

I am sure of one thing only.

To thrive in this world or the one I used to know,
to achieve my full potential,
to feel warmth again,

I need to

know that I am not alone.

Our feelings are valid,
they really are.
But,

> **we must desert the notion**
> **that we are alone.**

The *gateway to the sun*

bab al-shams   يـــاب التـمـس

is when you

> *desert the notion that you are alone.*

swan song

Let these bars and beats
lull you to sleep
and awake you with
the courage to be
a warrior of hope:

LIONHEART LULLABY

Shimmer down, shimmer down
simmer down, simmer down
tears are fallin'
like the leaves ain't in Texas.
Hate keeps on spreading
but love is infectious.
Be the one to protect us.
Be the one to connect us.

Hey, love, love, love!
Be a warrior of love.
We may be the prey
but let's pray to raise
lionhearted cubs, amen!
Southside Chicago!

Hey, love, love, love!

Compassion, the highest form of love,
reminds me of the supreme
inside each one of us.

We will be challenged,
life is a ballad.

Hey, **love**, love, love!

Hey, love, **love**, love!

Hey, love, love, **love.**

be well,
namaste.

quicksand to dunes

A side note, but not any less important. Finding a point of equity.

| | Buried in Quicksand —> Lifted by Dunes: commentary on the US education system and advice for society | |

We were born to succeed,
but we are not supported to succeed.

Indeed, what else can we do? I ask YOU.
What else can you do?
That is the question isn't it.

When we hit the quicksand, we will sink. And suffocation is inevitable. What if we were to never step in at all?

What if we were to step up?

Placing a child who bolts like a Porsche in the merciless depths of the Pacific when they were made for Highway 1, is setting a bud in need of blooming up for failure, a drowning of sorts, so much so, that they cannot ever get to where they should be.

But, never say never, right?

Placing a child who glides like a Bertram on a car-infested freeway is, ironically, prison.

And they will be stationary for as long as they are stationed.

And how will this child know that being themselves is the best thing they could hope to be when they are surrounded by the constant reminder that, in this environment, they cannot function as well as all the different people they see?

And they are forced to change—
for their survival.

Survival is not THRIVAL.

Place your child, the one *entrusted* to your *care*, in soil that nurtures their seed. And while yes,
it may be difficult to perceive,
you brought and cared for a unique seed
never before seen or heard by the world —
place them on a **dune** that is
deserving of their ingenuities.

A hill from where they can see the dips and curves
of the globe they make for themselves
and those around them.

About the Author

ANJALI SEBASTIAN, born on August 3, 2001, is an Indian-American lyricist, singer-songwriter, pianist, poet, voice artist, and yogi.

Anjali loves to harness the power of music with audiences and fellow song-writers, artists, performers, creators, and dreamers all around the world. Ever since she wrote her first full song at age nine, she has found great joy and courage by being involved in the creative music process.

Anjali's mantras in life are: "we are filled to overflow" and "loving someone encompasses loving one's journey."

To get to know more about and connect with Anjali, visit www.anjalisebastian.com.